Inside front cover and facing page

1894 OS map showing location of the palace.
The extent of the land acquired has been outlined upon it.
The dotted area was leased to give access.

The 1920 OS map, based on surveys made 1910-13.
Comparision with the 1894 map shows where terraced roads have been built.
Note the switchback and other facilities in the park.

PALACE ON THE HILL

*A HISTORY OF ALEXANDRA PALACE
AND PARK*

by
KEN GAY

Published by Hornsey Historical Society

1992

Hornsey Historical Society
136 Tottenham Lane,
London N8 7EL

First published 1992

ISBN 0 905794 08 7

Cover Design: by Richard Robertson
Production: Peter Curtis

Set in 10 point Times Roman, by Pennant Press

Printed and bound in Great Britain by
J.G. Bryson (Printer) Ltd.
156-162 High Road, East Finchley, London N2.

PALACE ON THE HILL

Alexandra Palace, set in its park, is a unique surviving example of the Victorian passion for large buildings and great enterprises. Constructed about six miles from London, it aimed to attract thousands to a People's Palace, offering them a wonderland of exhibits and events. Its chequered history since is a record of hope and failure, but still survival. High on its hill, and visible for miles, it has won an affectionate place in many people's hearts. How did this building and park come into existence, and why was its location so chosen?

The site

Alexandra Palace stands on what was Tottenham Wood Farm, some 400 acres of mainly pasture land, stretching between the Middlesex villages of Muswell Hill, Wood Green and Hornsey. The farm took its name from the wood which crowned the high lands in the western part of the ancient parish of Tottenham. Roque's map of Middlesex of 1754 depicts the wood as still occupying the area. During the 18th century it was cleared, all but 11 acres.

In 1789 the land was put up for auction, with the rest of his Tottenham estates by the Earl of Coleraine, then lord of the manor. The sale details are given in Robinson's *History of Tottenham* (1840) which describes it as:

'A freehold estate, consisting of Tottenham Wood, near to Muswell Hill, the principal part of which was then cleared and cultivated'.

The purchaser was Mr Mitchell, a tobacconist of Norton Folgate, London, who paid £11,400. Soon after the purchase Mr Mitchell 'built a good house on it' and laid out a considerable amount of money on improvements. Mr Mitchell's farmhouse was to survive until 1932, for most of its last four decades as the clubhouse for Muswell Hill golf club. Its portico still stands in Rhodes Avenue, N22 on the road between Muswell Hill and Bounds Green.

Tottenham Wood Farmhouse built circa 1790. Acquired with the farmlands, used from 1894 by the golf club, and demolished in 1932.

On Mr Mitchell's death Thomas Rhodes became proprietor. The name Rhodes was to become internationally famous through the activities in Africa of Cecil Rhodes (1853-1902). But Thomas Rhodes (1763-1856), a great uncle, would hardly have known the little boy, born in Bishops Stortford a few years before he died.

Thomas Rhodes built up Tottenham Wood Farm and aimed to have 1,000 cows, an ambition unrealised. Additional land was acquired by Rhodes in 1850 when the new Great Northern trunk railway bisected the Nightingale Hall estate, adjacent to his own on the east. Rhodes's farm stretched from this railway as far as Muswell Hill village and south to the Priory estate on the western edge of Hornsey village, to encompass some 450 acres.

This part of Middlesex was very little populated in the first half of the 19th century. Farming was dairy, pasture and hayfields. Increasingly, prosperous London traders and professionals built villas in the area. In addition institutions were established in the countryside, such as the almshouses and masonic school at Wood Green and the asylum to the north which still survives as Friern Barnet Hospital. Like Alexandra Palace after it, this 1851 building was erected on a hill sloping to the south, but was even vaster in size. Alexandra Palace was to be yet one more huge institutional building set in the countryside, transport to it made possible by the railway.

The Great Northern had begun operations in 1850, with trains running from the newly built Kings Cross station from 1852. The first stations then out of London were Hornsey and Colney Hatch (later renamed New Southgate). In 1859 a new station was opened between them called Wood Green (now Alexandra Palace). According to testimony by the general manager of the railway at an 1864 Commons enquiry into further railway proposals, the sum of £4,000 had been paid towards the cost of this new station by Mr Rhodes, the owner of the adjacent estate. 'They wanted to make it into a residential place and they subscribed the money in order to enhance the value of the land to make a station', he said.

Wood Green station was opened a few years after the death of Thomas Rhodes in 1856. Aged 93 he had outlived his son and his property went to his remaining family, the estate going to his grandchildren. His family included his son's widow and her children and two daughters, one of whom was married. The likelihood is that it was the family which had had the idea of using the farmlands to build villas. Or it might have part of a scheme, first publicised in 1858 to develop the land not only for villas but for the creation of a 'people's palace'.

The idea of a palace

Tottenham Wood farmlands were to be the focus of a grand idea, that of a Palace of the People, propagated by the architect Owen Jones (1809-76). The concept for this stemmed from the Great Exhibition of 1851. This event had celebrated the British achievements in manufacturing and trade which had followed from the so-called Industrial Revolution. The exhibition was copied by other world cities soon afterwards.

The 1851 exhibition had been held in Hyde Park, London in a glass and metal building designed by Paxton. Originally called The Palace of Industry, it was dubbed 'The Crystal Palace' by *Punch* magazine because of its pioneering glass construction. Involved in the interior decoration of the Paxton building was the architect Owen Jones. He was also among those responsible for its subsequent reconstruction between 1852-54 on a 200-acre site near a railway line at Sydenham, south London. Owen Jones was to make his name as a pioneer of Islamic colour and abstract patterns, and as author of an influential book *Grammar of Ornament* (1856). It can be said that Jones was the prime instigator of the Alexandra Palace.

Owen Jones's concept seems to have been for a building north of London similar to Crystal Palace in the south, also set in a rural area near a railway and served by a spur line. At some date Jones must have been in discussion with the Rhodes family about the acquisition of their property as the site for the scheme. For in December 1858 in St James's Vestry Hall, Piccadilly, Jones exhibited his drawings of his proposed 'Palace of the People, Muswell Hill'. A pamphlet accompanied the exhibition and read:

'The site selected for THE PALACE OF THE PEOPLE possesses peculiar advantages for the erection of a Building devoted to the Instruction and Amusement of the masses. It is situated on a great trunk railway, easily accessible by road from the most thickly populated districts of London, and from its elevated position commands the most extensive and beautiful views in all directions.

The site, moreover, possesses an inestimable advantage in that its most elevated portion is nearly in the centre of the grounds, so that not only will the Building itself be well seen from all sides, but from each of its fronts most beautiful views will be obtained. The favourable nature of the site has therefore guided the Architect in the general distribution of his plan.

In designing the Building, the Architect has endeavoured to combine the objects which the Promoters have in view, viz "to afford on a large scale the means of Intellectual Improvement and Physical Recreation to the masses", with such features of Design as should render the Building itself attractive, a point of great importance to a Self-Supporting Institution.'

Describing the proposed building Owen Jones wrote in his pamphlet:

'The arrangement of Two Naves separates also naturally that portion of the Building which may be devoted to Commercial purposes. Thus in one Nave there may be a permanent Exhibition of the Works of Industry and the Objects of Commerce; and in the other, the Arts and Sciences, which direct and embellish the Products of Industry, may find their appropriate home. .... To render such an Institution thoroughly available to the instruction of the masses, the Architect felt it to be necessary to provide a Lecture-theatre.......this theatre would contain ten thousand people, and he believes that every one might see and hear distinctly..... Beneath the platform on which the Lecture-theatre stands is the Railway Station, in which passengers would arrive under cover, and ascend to the ground-floor.... a similar provision is made for those visitors who arrive in carriages ....'

Surviving prints of Owen Jones's proposed building show a truly remarkable structure, a crystal palace which would have been a fine addition to the hill-top. City interest was aroused and in June 1859 Owen Jones was with Lord Brougham when he inaugurated the proposed site in the presence of some 200

4

The Palace of the People
which Owen Jones proposed should be built at Muswell Hill.

people and the band of the Coldstream Guards. But sufficient finance was not obtained to launch the project and the Great Northern Palace company was dissolved. Owen Jones's magnificent glass design never materialised. Sadly another glass building designed by Jones for St Cloud near Paris was also never built. But his ideas for a people's palace, with a large hall accomodating thousands, served by a railway were eventually to be implemented.

Realisation of the idea

The idea of a palace set in parkland did not die. Another company was formed, the farmlands bought and on 23rd July 1863 the Alexandra Park Company opened their venture to the public. The launch was celebrated by a fete in the grounds of Tottenham Wood farmhouse and in the Grove, acquired at the same time.

The Grove estate, adjacent to the Rhodes farmlands, was an ancient estate on the side of Muswell Hill, empty since the death of William Block, the last occupant, in 1861. Purchase of this land gave an exit for the new park on to the main road. Among the notable tenants of the Grove had been Topham Beauclerk, an illegitimate descendant of Charles II by Nell Gwynne. Many 18th

5

century people of eminence visited him at the Grove, including his friend Dr Samuel Johnson. A tree-lined avenue in the Grove is known as Dr Johnson's walk.

In Topham Beauclerk's hands the Grove was a splendid place, with landscaped grounds, an observatory with a resident astronomer, and a laboratory for chemical experiments. Tickets to view had to be issued because of the many unvited callers. Today the ambience of a gentleman's estate can still be perceived in its ten acres, though the house was demolished in the early 1870s. It is in contrast with the main body of the park, created on cow pastures.

Opened in July 1863, the name which the park, and subsequently the palace, received is a chance of history. It was on 7th March 1863 that a young Danish princess landed at Gravesend (a fine painting of the occasion hangs in the National Portrait Gallery) to be married three days later to the heir to the throne, the Prince of Wales, later Edward VII. Their marriage occurred just over four months before the park was opened. The name was chosen as a tribute to Princess Alexandra (1844-1925) later to become Queen Alexandra on the death of Queen Victoria. If Edward's fancy had alighted on Alexandra a year or so later the park might well have been known instead as, say, Victoria Park.

The 1862 exhibition building in South Kensington, designed by Captain Francis Fowke. Notable features, such as this Exhibition Road entrance portico, were to be reused at Muswell Hill. (Courtesy of the Board of Trustees of the V & A).

The first palace built on the hill was very different from Jones's glass-dream. It was constructed from building materials from an 1862 exhibition building in South Kensington, which had stood for a year on a site later used for the Natural History Museum. The 1862 exhibition had made no surplus receipts and the building remained the property of the joint contracting builders John Kelk and Lucas Brothers. The transportable materials were purchased for some £100,000 and brought to Muswell Hill. The civil engineer and architect Alfred Meeson (1808-1885) then used them for the palace which he designed along with Kelk's associate architect John Johnson (1807-1879). Meeson had worked with Sir Charles Barry in the construction of the Palace of Westminster, and for Kelk had produced the working drawings for the construction of the 1862 exhibition building designed by Francis Fowke.

Construction of the palace, undertaken by Kelk and Lucas, seems to have begun fairly quickly although the building was not to be opened until 1873. In 1865 the Alexandra Park Company went into liquidation and was replaced in 1866 by two new companies. The Muswell Hill Estate company was responsible for the lands. The Alexandra Palace Company leased part of these lands for the park and palace. This has been said to be the first formal naming of the building as Alexandra Palace.

The first Alexandra Palace built 1864-66 from the South Kensington exhibition building materials. Designed by Meeson and Johnson and opened in 1873. In the foreground is Rectory Road,   and Middle Lane, rebuilt post war with council flats. (Courtesy of Greater London Photograph Library).

7

In September 1866 the *North London News* reported:

'The magnificent structure now in course of construction on the very top of Muswell Hill is fast approaching completion. The contractors have twelve thousand men engaged. The works were commenced in September 1865 and have been carried through with unabated energy throughout the monetary crisis.....the Great Northern Railway have already purchased the Edgware and Highgate Railway by means of which they will obtain a second line to the Palace'.

Bringing the masses to the palace was seen from the beginning as important, as Jones's pamphlet had indicated, and the railway was the means by which they were to come, aided by some provision for carriage folk. Wood Green station on the Great Northern Railway was on the eastern perimeter of the farmlands and a steep uphill climb faced those who made their way from the station to the site of the palace. Jones's idea of a railway line right into the palace itself was seen as the answer to the problem.

Land was purchased from 1867 and the line built 1871-73. From the north side of the palace its route was through the park via the Grove estate to the side of Muswell Hill where a station was built next to the Green Man. The line then crossed a valley by a seven-arch viaduct (still standing over St James's Lane) to circle round the north side of Highgate Woods and to join Highgate station.

Highgate station was on the Edgware, Highgate & London Railway which had begun operations in August 1867 as a branch line from what is now Finsbury Park station on the GNR. Before operations began the EH & L railway had been purchased by the Great Northern.

It was the Great Northern which built the branch line from Highgate to the palace, taking over powers obtained in 1864 by the Edgware, Highgate & London Railway to run a line terminating at Muswell Hill on the boundary of Alexandra Park and in 1866 to run a railway through the park to the palace.

The preamble to the 1866 Muswell Hill Estate & Railways Act noted that the landowners, the Muswell Hill Estate company had leased to the Alexandra Palace company for 999 years the land which was 'being laid out in an ornamental manner and for public resort and recreation' whilst another part was 'being laid out as building ground'. In the 1870s the estate company was to sell the freehold interest of the leased land to the Alexandra Palace Company.

Although the railway line from Highgate to Muswell Hill was owned and operated by the Great Northern Railway the portion of the line through Alexandra Park itself belonged to the Muswell Hill Estate Company. When the palace opened this section was worked as well by the GNR as the Estate Company did not possess train stock.

When the line was opened in 1873 travellers by steam train to the palace could thus make their way from Kings Cross via Finsbury Park and Highgate. Most visitors bought a one-shilling return fare from Kings Cross which included admission. The expensive charge of 2d single fare from Muswell Hill station to the palace was charged by the estate company.

Whilst the palace was being built a race course was opened in the park in June 1868 on the flatter land to the south, towards the Priory estate and Hornsey village. A grandstand was built at the same time. The racecourse was to remain operational for 102 years, till 1970. When it was closed the grandstand was demolished and some 40 acres added to the park. The racecourse was to provide useful income, especially in the early years. Large crowds attended, with trotting races another feature. Edward VII was among those who came and a local pub was named The Victoria (now the Victoria Stakes). After the second world war meetings were reduced to six a year.

Eventually the palace was ready and on 24th May 1873 it was opened by Queen Victoria, on her birthday. A report in *The Illustrated London News* of 31st May, 1873 said:

'The opening last Saturday of the Alexandra Palace and Park, at Muswell hill beyond Hornsey, on the north side of London was a pleasant festival to many thousands of visitors...The grounds are situated in the most agreeable part of Middlesex, exactly six miles from Charing Cross, but amidst rural scenery of delightful freshness, variety and beauty. They have an extent of 220 acres, laid out in park and garden, on the summit of a range of green hills, adorned with flourishing oaks and elms.....The entire estate here belonging to the Company is 600 acres, the greater part of which is reserved for building mansions or villas'.

'The Alexandra Palace has been constructed by Messrs. Kelk and Lucas from the designs of Messrs Meeson and Johnson, architects. It is an edifice stately and dignified as well as elegant....The architectural style is Italian...The new line of railway from Kings-cross to the Alexandra Palace is most convenient, giving access to it by a station platform directly beneath the main entrance, with an ascent by a few steps to the central transept'.

In the first two weeks the Palace was visited by over 120,000 people, mostly coming by railway. But Meeson and Johnson's building was to be short lived. Sixteen days later, on Monday 9th June 1873, the great palace was reduced to a smouldering ruin.

The first fire and the second palace

The fire which began about half an hour after the palace had opened started on the roof but seems never to have been satisfactorily explained. A worker

9

soldering zinc on the roof was using a coke and charcoal fire pot with soldering irons, but he claimed that he left his pot in a cast-iron box when he left the roof, and that the fire started elsewhere. Also on the roof had been five painters at work on the dome. Fortunately no visitors were killed but three palace workers died; one was struck fifty yards from the building by falling debris, and was to die in the Great Northern Hospital four days later.

The fire was seen as a catastrophe, widely reported and illustrated by steel engravings made from sketches and photographs. Concern was expressed about the need for fire prevention measures and the inadequacy of the water supply to deal with the fire on the day. These factors were taken into account when a new palace was designed. For on the same day the company directors agreed to rebuild as soon as practicable, and to continue to run the planned outside events.

This time the palace was designed by the architect John Johnson who had worked with Meeson on the first palace. Kelk and Lucas made a £232,000 tender to rebuild and despite inadequate insurance on the first building reconstruction went ahead. Using the same site and some of the original materials (it has been said that some features from the 1862 South Kensington exhibition building can still be seen in the rebuilt palace) John Johnson built a larger, redesigned building over seven acres in extent. Its final cost was £417,128. Thus was bequeathed to the future an extensive structure requiring considerable heating and maintenance.

The shell of the first palace, burnt 16 days after it had been opened in 1873 by Queen Victoria. (Courtesy of Roy Tremlett).

10

The second Alexandra Palace, designed by Johnson and opened in 1875. This aerial 1930 view shows the north facade and turrets still in situ on each of the four corner towers. (Courtesy of Bruce Castle).

Johnson's building, which survives today in modified form following its reconstruction after the 1980 fire, seemed to lack the architectural attractiveness of the first palace. Described in disparaging terms over the years, it nevertheless was the huge familiar building which so many generations have come to know. It can be seen from far around and many have the same regard for it and its huge shape as others do for an old and unprepossessing aunt, held in the affection which long years of familiarity can create.

The new building was opened on 1st May 1875 by the Lord Mayor of London, with 21,000 people present. On the Whit Monday following some 94,000 came. Mostly they travelled by rail. Unfortunately a derailment in the Copenhagen tunnel leading into Kings Cross in the evening blocked the line. Many got off the trains at Holloway station, whilst others slept the night through on them. Journeys by train even then were subject to unexpected delays.

Johnson's plan for the rebuilt palace included the large hall which had originally been envisaged by Owen Jones. It was 386 feet long and 184 feet wide and designed to seat 12,000 people with 2,000 more in the orchestra stalls below the organ.

The Willis organ was a great feature of the palace. It was built by Henry Willis (1821-1901) who had established organ works in Camden Town. Willis built

The central hall with the Willis organ. Suspended from the ceiling are the gas lights which lit the hall. (Courtesy of Roy Tremlett).

Exhibition hall with typical Victorian display cases. (Courtesy of Bruce Castle).

organs for Gloucester Cathedral, the Crystal Palace, the Royal Albert Hall St George's Hall, Liverpool, Blenheim Palace and other places. The first organ built for Alexandra Palace by Willis had been burnt down in the fire, with Willis himself escaping only just in time.

The new organ outstripped any built by other makers and was the principal organ in the country in size, design and equipment. It was driven by two steam engines with vast bellows in the basement. Saving and restoring the organ after the second world war was an important *leitmotif* in saving the palace itself from being demolished. (There has been an appeal seeking cash to complete its restoration from the time when rebuilding of the palace after the 1980 fire began.)

The accompanying illustration shows the ground floor plan in 1934. The Great Hall is the central feature. This replaced the domed central transept of the first palace. The hall ran between huge gables on both north and south sides which were saved from the original structure and probably derive from the 1862 exhibition materials. Considered to be good examples of neo-Florentine early renaissance design, they are still *in situ.* Outside, on the north side a flight of steps formed the main entrance to the restored palace. From the steps a wide avenue led though the park northwards. Today this part of the park has been built over and the entrance avenue has become a suburban road called The Avenue, lined mainly with Edwardian houses. The steps remain but are not in general use.

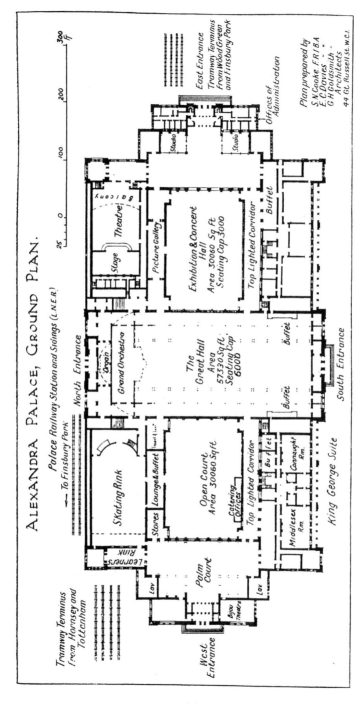

ALEXANDRA PALACE, GROUND PLAN.

Palace Railway Station and Sidings (L.N.E.R.)

To Finsbury Park

North Entrance

East Entrance

Tramway Terminus from Wood Green and Finsbury Park

Offices of Administration

Plan prepared by
S. N. Cooke. F.R.I.B.A
E. C. Davies "
G. H. Goldsmith "
Architects
44 Gt. Russell st. w.c.1.

Studio

Studio

Picture Gallery

Balcony

Theatre

Stage

Exhibition & Concert Hall
Area 30060 Sq Ft
Seating Cap. 3000

Top Lighted Corridor

Buffet

Organ

Grand Orchestra

The Great Hall
Area 57330 sq ft.
Seating Cap. 6000

Buffet

Buffet

South Entrance

Skating Rink

Stores

Lounge & Buffet

Open Court
Area 30060 Sq ft

Catering Offices

Top Lighted Corridor

Buffet

Buffet

Connaught Rm.

King George Suite

Learner's Rink

Lav

Palm Court

Bijou Theatre

Lav

Middlesex Rm.

West Entrance

Tramway Terminus from Hornsey and Tottenham

Ground plan of the second palace showing the great central hall and other areas.
(Courtesy of Bruce Castle).

14

The hall was flanked on each side by courtyards, probably to act as fire breaks should another conflagration occur. But before the opening, the courtyard on the east side of the Great Hall had been roofed over and was labelled Bazaar Department on Johnson's plan. This is the area which in 1990 was opened as an ice skating rink. The courtyard on the west side was known as the Italian Garden. It contained a large fountain now to be seen in a rose garden in the park east of the palace. When the palace was reconstructed after the 1980 fire the Italian Garden was converted into the West exhibition hall.

Beyond the Italian Garden on the west side was a conservatory area filled with unusual plants. After the 1980 fire it was restored, its fine roof reglazed, and is known as the Palm Court. By the west entrance was an exhibition and lecture room, converted in the post-1980 fire restoration into the Londesborough Room (named after the collection of arms and armour formed by Lord Londesborough which had once been housed here). Also by the west entrance was a library and reading room in the area occupied by the Phoenix Bar since 1988.

At the four corners of the building were towers, with pointed roofs. These contained tanks of water also to help fight fires. Four other tanks of water stood near the central hall. Steam pumps from the New River Company reservoirs (subsequently Thames Water Board) were to provide water.

On the north-east corner of the building was included a theatre, built almost to the dimensions of Drury Lane Theatre. Somewhat modernised in the 1920s this Victorian-age auditorium, with some of its original stage-machinery still survives, but finance was not available in the post-1980 reconstruction to restore or convert it.

On the north-east corner was a concert hall with another Willis organ. Later this area was adapted as a roller-skating rink. This was very popular, especially with young people, before and after the Second World War. In the 1980s restoration it became an area used by delivery transport as a service yard for the new exhibition halls.

The ground plan also shows exhibition galleries, banqueting and other refreshment rooms, and offices. Beneath the palace were vast cellars used for kitchens, maintenance, storage and other purposes. On the north side the lower level of the palace was used for the palace's own railway station but platforms outside were to be used later.

Activities at the Palace and Park in Victorian and Edwardian times

An extraordinary range of activities was to be carried out in both palace and park in succeeding decades after the opening, too many to describe in detail. Programmes and prospectuses survive which show almost every kind of entertainment.

In April 1876, for example, the Alexandra Palace Company published its 'Prospective Arrangements' for the 1876-77 season. After distribution of works of art in the Alexandra Palace Art Union on Monday, May 1st, an opening day on Saturday, May 6th would include a 'grand concert', 'great flower show', and a 'grand display of fireworks' with 'the entire band of the Grenadier Guards' in attendance. A special fete to celebrate the return of HRH the Prince of Wales from India was to be arranged.

Planned for the season were two Italian Concerts, one with Madame Adelina Patti, two Italian operas, a national music festival, three ballad operas, open air musical performances in the Grove, Saturday popular concerts, morning performances of operas by Mr Carl Rosa's company, readings and dramatic performances by Mr Jefferson and Mr Toole in the lecture theatre.

As well as showing the Londesborough collection of arms and armour, the picture galleries would be open, with a changing collection of paintings as well as sculpture. The Art Union Prize for the year was a Parian bust of Ophelia by W. Calder Marshall RA, of which 'only a limited number will be issued'. A loan collection of state and civic awards, supplemented by insignia of chivalric decorations and presentation jewels, was to be on display for the season.

Monkey house and zoo, were notable attractions at the palace. The Palm Court hosed a lofty aviary. (Courtesy of Rag Raghavan).

16

Horticulturists were told about the 'grand flower show', the great 'rose show', and the autumn flower shows. In the grounds would be fireworks, race meetings, American trotting matches, bicycle races, the great annual horse show, pony races, a dog show, pigeon flights, shows of cats, rabbits and guinea pigs, athletic sports, a great Scotch fete and annual fetes arranged by eight organisations. The gymnasium would reopen for the season in May.

The Banqueting Hall and the grand dining hall would be available, also 'retiring rooms' for both gentlemen and ladies. A police office and metropolitan fire brigade station were at the south entrance of the central hall, and a volunteer fire brigade, consisting of members of the company's staff, had been organised. By arrangement with the Post Office 'the Alexandra Palace is now placed in direct telegraphic communication with the Metropolis and all parts of the Kingdom, as well as with Foreign Countries', with the telegraph office at the eastern entrance. The London Stereoscopic company 'had been entrusted with the sole right of photography, and suitable studios have been provided for the purpose'.

In 1882 an 'Alexandra Palace Daily Programme', sold for one penny, detailed four pages of entertainments for the August Bank Holiday Monday. A twelve hour programme running from 10 am was provided. This included organ performances; a circus in the concert room; a tea-pot making exhibition in the Bazaar; 'clown cricketers' on the cricket ground; a band in the Banqueting Hall; 'cookery entertainments' in the lecture room; the Alexandra Palace Band in the central hall; feeding the lions in the concert room; concerts of Irish, Scotch and English songs; a band on the banks of the triple lakes; Myers's 'Great Hippodrome' with pony races and elephants in the north park; variety entertainments in the theatre; British Army Quadrilles in the Grove, with drums and fifes of the 1st Middlesex Engineers and pipers of the Scots Guards; a 'pedestrian meeting and obstacle races' on the sports ground; ballet in the theatre; 'Assault at Arms', including foils, Indian clubs and boxing in the park; a Circus; a balloon ascent by Mr Barker in the south park; a giant Punch and Judy show on the north terrace; a play 'Streets of London' in the theatre; a grand display of fireworks by Mr James Pain; and a shadow pantomime.

Other attractions detailed in the 1882 daily programme included 'Garibaldi and Mazzini Relics'; a panorama of The Siege of Sevastopol; a chance to see ice being brought out of the refrigerator behind the organ; an exhibition of food stuffs; a room illustrating the 'wonderful invention of luminous paint'; a rose fair and mart; and the chance to see Iros, the 'marvellous Aerial Globe Walker' in the central hall. The refreshment department offered either a shilling or 1s 6d tea in the saloons, or snacks and drinks in tents or in the Banqueting Hall in the park. Season tickets could be purchased for the Palace at 3 shillings monthly, children half price.

17

The boating lake has always been one of the more popular places in Alexandra Park. (Courtesy of Roy Tremlett).

As these programmes indicate, leisure and entertainment events of all kinds were carried on in Alexandra Park during the season. Some 220 acres in extent, the park had been laid out by Alexander McKenzie. Facilities and features included an open air swimming pool (near the main railway and reservoirs); a Japanese village brought from an exhibition in Vienna and put up by Japanese workmen in the area now occupied by the Grove car park (the village burnt down in 1897 and the site was levelled in 1909); a large Swiss Chalet (burnt down in 1898) next to the Japanese village; a string of ornamental lakes on the line of present day Grove Avenue; boating facilities; tennis courts; funfair fixtures; and other amenities.

As we have seen, activities in the grounds included firework displays, rallies, bicycle matches, trotting, pigeon races, cricket matches, kite-flying, horse shows and open air musical performances. The park was also used for various aerial displays. Notable among the latter was parachute jumping from a balloon, with an American known as Professor JS Baldwin being very popular. Baldwin ascended whilst clutching a rope beneath his balloon. Landing points were not always as intended. Missing the trunk railway Baldwin was known to have landed in the Printers' Almshouses grounds in Wood Green, in Stroud Green Road, Highgate Woods, and on one occasion on the roof of the local authority offices in Southwood Lane, Highgate where he was presented with a £5 surety bill to cover damages. In all Baldwin made 98 descents, including one from the roof of the central hall. It was to see Baldwin that Princess Alexandra made the first of her two visits to the Palace.

A notable parachutist who made her first drop in the grounds of the park was a seventeen year old girl from New Southgate known as Dolly Shepherd. In 1904, in the park, she met the air pioneers SF Cody (brother of Buffalo Bill) and AE Gaudrion. For the latter she ascended into the air some 2,000 feet or more hanging from a hot air balloon before parachuting down. Good looking Dolly Shepherd continued jumping until 1912, when she had a premonition she ought to stop. The successful development of early aeroplanes also meant the end of the balloon era. Born in 1886, Dolly Shepherd was to live to the age of 97.

The Palace and Park from 1875 to 1900

Irish jaunting cars were in attendance at the Wood Green entrance to convey visitors to the palace and round the park, at fixed charges, according to the 1876 prospectus. This provision was no doubt intended for those who arrived at Wood Green station on the main Great Northern line, and is carried on today by the free buses which exhibition organisers lay on for the same journey, to encourage and facilitate attendance.

Getting to the palace has always been a problem and good attendance was necessary for the building's success. Other railway promoters planned lines but the only one built was that by the Great Eastern to a station misleadingly called Palace Gates. This was about a mile from the palace and a few hundred yards further east than the Great Northern's Wood Green station, adding a further distance to walk before the steep uphill climb.

Opened in January 1878 this new line ran across Green Lanes through Tottenham and south to Liverpool Street. The greater importance of this railway was its role in helping the village of Wood Green change into a London suburb of terraced streets. The station on Green Lanes was handy for the new estate of Noel Park, built in the 1880s, and was to lead to the development of Green Lanes into the busy shopping thoroughfare known as Wood Green High Road. The railway was to be operated for passenger traffic until 1963. After operations ceased part of the Wood Green track was used for the development of a new shopping centre, opened in 1980.

As far as the Palace and Park were concerned it was only on Sundays and Bank Holidays that the trippers and leisure seekers came in great numbers. Originally conceived by Owen Jones to cater for the education and leisure interests of the masses, the concept of a People's Palace was flawed by thr fact that the masses had very little leisure. Six regular Bank Holidays were established by Act of Parliament in 1875 but these were not enough to bring sufficient people. The vast building needed heat and maintenance and employees' wages had to be paid. Some managements reduced costs by opening only from spring to autumn but the financial problems remained overwhelming. The entire history of the palace from the beginning till now is based on the struggle to maintain a constant flow of visitors and to generate income sufficient to cover capital and running costs.

Under private ownership in the last quarter of the 19th century, this effort failed time and time again. In 1877 ownership passed to the London Financial Association who (in co-partnership with Kelk and Lucas) bought it from the Alexandra Palace Co. The Association leased to different managements but success was elusive. In the period 1875-1900 there were eight managements, five of which went into liquidation. In the last quarter of the 19th century the palace was open for little more than ten years and closed completely form September 1889 to March 1898.

The London Financial Association sought to cut its losses by disposing of the palace and park over this period but was not successful. In 1877 they acquired parliamentary powers to dispose of eighty acres north of the building so that it could be sold for housing. This area included the boating lake, the triple lakes (now Grove Avenue), and the northern entrance, now The Avenue. In 1878 and in the 1880s come plots were sold and roads laid out but the time was not ripe in Muswell Hill for urban development. This had to wait for the arrival of the developer James Edmondson in 1896 who replaced villas in a rural setting with the nucleus of Muswell Hill Broadway and surrounding avenues.

Efforts to improve rail communication were not to have positive effects. In 1886 parliamentary powers were obtained to create the Muswell Hill & Palace Railway as a separate body from its owner the Muswell Hill Estate Company. This enabled the palace terminus to operate as a public railway station, with an improved building on the north side. It was hoped to attract local residents to travel but the sparse population made this unrealistic. During the periods of continuous closure of the palace the station remained mostly closed as well. In 1898 when surburban development began locally it became continuously operative.

Meanwhile the rural aspect of the surrounding ancient parishes of Hornsey and Tottenham was being destroyed by terraced housing in the 1880s and 1890s. Wood Green, on the east side of the park outgrew its village beginnings and in 1888 became independent as a local authority from Tottenham. The result of urbanisation was that the value to the community of the park as an open space increased immensely. Efforts were made by HR Williams, energetic chairman of Hornsey Local Board to save it from housing development as he had helped save Highgate Woods. In 1887 he proposed that it be purchased for a public park as a Jubilee Memorial to Queen Victoria, then fifty years on the throne.

These efforts got nowhere, as did other attempts by the London Financial Association to sell off the palace and park at auction or otherwise dispose of it. Proposed purchasers were the Blue Coat School, the Salvation Army and promoters of a sanitorium. Open space was preserved beyond the housing plots on the north side of the park on the former farmlands (originally earmarked for housing) by the creation of a golf course. Muswell Hill Golf Club, one of the first two golf clubs in the London area, in 1893 acquired substantial acres. They rented the still surviving Tottenham Wood farmhouse as a club house and remained in it till 1932 when they built a new

Alexandra Palace rail terminus was on the north side of the building.

clubhouse on the course and the farmhouse was demolished. With an adjacent 14 acre recreation ground (1926), an area of allotments gardens and a small remnant of the original wood, mostly on the former farmlands a valuable green lung was obtained. Encompassing the park this stretched north across the golf course and the Bounds Green Brook valley lands (from the late 1920s the route of the North Circular Road) to meet with the Friern Barnet hospital grounds at Colney Hatch.

Under public ownership

Public ownership of the park and palace, preserving them for the benefit of the community was achieved under the 1900 Alexandra Park and Palace (Public Purposes) Act. In February 1901 responsibility was placed in the hands of trustees drawn from the consortium of local authorities which had purchased 173 acres, including the 10 acre Grove and 28 acres of leasehold land which had comprised the racecourse and Hornsey entrance area. The purchase price of £150,000 also included the palace. An additional £15,000 was given for another 18 acres on the north side which included the boating lake which was intended to be built over.

Henry Burt JP of Hornsey Urban District Council and Middlesex County Council, the man who had done much to promote the installation of public libraries in Hornsey, was a leading figure in seeing through the purchase. He was ably assisted by Sir Ralph Littler KC of Middlesex County Council (who lived nearby at Broomfield House, in

21

Sir Ralph Littler and Mr Henry Burt (Courtesy of Roy Tremlett).

what is now Broomfield Park). The initial deposit for the purchase was hurriedly put up by Hornsey councillors themselves to secure it. The urban district councils which made up the consortium were Hornsey, Friern Barnet, Wood Green, Tottenham, Finchley, and Islington, with Middlesex County Council. Other councils which subsequently contributed towards the cost of extensions and renovations included Southgate, Edmonton, Finsbury, Stoke Newington, Enfield and the City of London. The idea has always been to have a regional park, catering for the populations in the surrounding areas.

On May 18th, 1901 there was a formal opening by the Lord Lieutenant of Middlesex, the Duke of Bedford. A short while earlier Edward had become King and a telegram of good wishes was received from Alexandra, now Queen. Around this time lands on the north-east side of the park finally succumbed to the builder. The area between Alexandra Park Road and Albert Road was covered by terraced roads. On the north-west side other new roads joined The Avenue to Colney Hatch Lane with suburban homes, made in good Edwardian mould of red brick and stone dressing. Churches were built to serve the new population. The palace no longer stood in the centre of undeveloped land.

New transport arrangements helped to make the palace more viable. From December 1905 an electric tramway went from Turnpike Lane, Wood Green to the foot of Muswell Hill and then by single deck car to the west end of the palace. From April 1906 another tramway connected the east end of the palace with Wood Green

A single decker tram on its way out of the park towards Priory Road and Wood Green. (Courtesy of Rag Raghavan).

via Station Road. An entrance to the park from Dukes Avenue was created at this time to allow local residents more easy access to the tram service. When in 1938 the trams were replaced by buses their routes were to become a through road in the park used by motor vehicles. By 1914 petrol buses were running as regular services between Muswell Hill Broadway and Highgate and Finsbury Park. These routes were seriously to affect the income of the steam railway to the palace. At that time the tube railway operated only as far as Highgate (Archway) and Finsbury Park.

Under public ownership programmes of entertainments continued each year. Flower shows, concerts in the Grove, amateur boxing championships, poultry shows, organ recitals, music by school choirs and orchestras, and firework displays were regular events. New works by Elgar were played such as the *Coronation Ode* (1901) and *Dream of Gerontius* (1904). *The Messiah, Elijah* and *Hiawatha* were staged. Artists over the years were to include Kreisler the violinist and the singers Dame Clara Butt, John McCormack and Peter Dawson. The American composer Sousa and his band and Sir Henry Wood and the Queens Hall Orchestra were notable visitors. Meetings in the Great Hall organised by the Liberal Party heard speeches by Asquith, Campbell-Bannerman, Lloyd George and Winston Churchill.

Switchback installed in the park in 1902 near the east end of the palace. (Courtesy of Bruce Castle).

The palace and park were used in 1902 as quarters for 2,500 colonial troops attending Edward VII's coronation. In 1905 Dr Barton finally flew the airship which for some years he had been constructing in the park. Its first flight was its last. In 1907 the Prince and Princess of Wales (later to be King George V and Queen Mary) visited the palace.

Sports were promoted, with a piece of parkland near Redston Road drained and fenced in 1909 in cooperation with Hornsey Borough Council to make a playing field for local elementary school children. In 1909 an indoor bowling club was formed and housed in the palace; it still survived in the 1990s. Sports were a particular concern of Councillor EW Sloper who took over as chairman of the trustees in 1910. Further improvements were made, such as new tennis courts near the boating lake, and plans were made for a stadium, but these were frustrated by the outbreak of war in 1914. Under Sloper's guidance the fortunes of the palace and park improved but capital was in short supply and difficulties continued.

The First World War changed the situation, temporarily, with the palace used from 1914 as a temporary transit camp for Belgian refugees, fleeing their country in the face of the German invasion. Some 38,000 passed through before March 1915 when their use of the palace was ended. It was to see the refugees that Queen Alexandra, now as Queen Mother, made her second visit to the palace.

24

Subsequently the palace and park was used as an internment camp. In 1916 there were over 2,200 prisoners of war, including 1,600 German and some 700 Austrian soldiers. The rent-free use of the property by the government persisted after the 1918 end to the war. Civil servants were housed in the palace and the park was not reopened to the public until March 1920. The palace itself was not handed back until 1922. One gain from the war-time period was the improvements made in the park by the prisoners, for which the Trustees paid. These included replacing the old elms in the Grove which had made up Dr Johnson's Walk, and making a promenade around the lake and an outdoor bowling green.

Alderman Edwin Sloper
chairman of the trustees and honorary secretary and manager from 1910 till his death in 1921. His efforts cleared off the palace debts.
(Courtesy of Roy Tremlett).

Between the wars

In 1923, on the fiftieth anniversary of the first palace, large commemorative plaques, still to be seen *in situ* in 1992, were placed on each side of a Great Hall entrance on the south terrace to mark the services of Henry Burt and Edwin Sloper.

The 1920s and 1930s saw different managers attempting to keep the palace activities going and to make the venture economically viable. For a short period MacQueen Pope (later to be well known as a theatre historian) became general manager. Changes were made to the theatre auditorium to promote this as a stage venue. Concerts and events of all kinds were held, with well known singers of the day engaged. Open air performances were given in the Grove. National scout rallies were held in the park. Kennel Club shows were held. In 1927 the North London exhibition was held as a new venture. Its success meant it became an annual event. The skating rink in the palace and sports such as cricket and football became attractions of particular note. Sunday was the most popular day but it needed special events to bring crowds in in large numbers.

From 1929 the famous Willis organ was restored and converted from steam to electric power. A new permanent resident organist, Reginald Goss-Custard was appointed. An earlier organist had been GD Cunningham. Visiting organist Marcel Dupré declared the organ to be the finest in Europe. Other organists who played included Thalben Ball and Reginald Foort (who was to make his name on the cinema organ at this time). Sir Henry Wood gave his services free at a 1938 concert to celebrate alterations to the organ pitch, with Isobel Baillie among the distinguished soloists.

In 1934 came a decision which was to make Alexandra Palace globally famous. The trustees rented the south-east end of the building to the BBC. A suitable high point was needed for the transmission of television pictures, and in 1935 a mast was built on the south-east tower. This famous television mast, in slightly reduced form, still survives. Internal areas were converted for studios and transmission. On 2nd November 1936, as a blue plaque at the foot of the south-east tower records, the world's first regular high definition public television service was inaugarated at Alexandra Palace.

The BBC initially experimented with two rival transmission systems, that developed by the famous Scots inventor James Logie Baird and an alternative

BBC studio at Alexandra Palace where the world's first regular high definition television service was pioneered from 1936 onwards. (Courtesy of Bruce Castle).

developed by Marconi-EMI. It was the latter which was finally selected. The initial two hours of daily transmissions could be seen within a radius of about 25 miles, that is by those able to afford the high-price receivers. One of my own boyhood memories is standing one winter night before the war looking into a shop window where the flickering blue screen some ten inches in height was showing a musical entertainment.

Alexandra Palace was to be the home of a new form of popular entertainment. From these beginnings the electronic theatre has spread to every continent in the world. The studios where these developments began — the idea of a public television service received in the domestic home — are still there. But interest in preserving them in recent years has been restricted to a few enthusiasts, despite their historical importance. Ally Pally's name however is written into cultural history.

The inter-war period was still a time of financial struggle. Debts had to be paid off and the government refused appeals for aid. Some councillors considered the palace should be demolished. Victorian architecture was not fashionable and in a contemporary magazine the author JB Priestley described the building as hideous.

The coming of the second world war in 1939 meant the end of activities for the duration. Belgian refugees came back to the palace for a second time, as well as troops home from Dunkirk. The palace avoided major bombing but in 1944 a flying bomb on the north side in The Avenue damaged the roof above the organ. In 1946-47 the organ was partly dismantled and stored.

Post war changes

It was 1957 before the Great Hall was restored, redecorated and reopened. The North London and other exhibitions were staged once more and conferences and banquets held in the Palace Suite. The roller-skating rink continued in use.

The palace's fortunes overall might have been revitalised after the war if a pre-war transport scheme had come to fruition. This had been the plan to electrify the branch railway to the palace and to make it part of the Northern line tube system. Most of the work had been undertaken before the war but had not been quite completed. Highgate underground station was opened in 1940 with the northern line operating to High Barnet (and to Mill Hill in 1941 to serve the barracks there) but the Alexandra Palace branch remained unfinished. After the war the decision was taken to abandon the further project, despite the huge capital investment that had been made.

The steam railway continued to operate but the local bus services to Finsbury Park, Highgate and Bounds Green and Wood Green tube stations (opened 1932) offered a more favoured way of travelling to London. Passenger services on the steam railway finally terminated in July 1954. Eventually the branch line track was taken up and most of the route became part of Haringey's Parkland Walk, a linear park walkable most of the way from Muswell Hill to Finsbury Park.

A significant change in public ownership of the palace took place in the mid-1960s. The 1963 London Government Act reorganised local councils, joining the boroughs of Hornsey, Wood Green and Tottenham to form the London Borough of Haringey and enlarged the London county area to form the Greater London Council, absorbing Middlesex county at the same time. The Minister of Housing and Local Government awarded control of the palace and park to the Greater London Council. The 1966 Alexandra Park and Palace Order defined the details of the change.

Public consultation was a feature of the GLC tenure with demolition of the palace considered as one possibility. Replies in 1974 indicated that many people wanted the palace and park retained and improved.

In 1971, during GLC tenure, the banqueting hall built in 1864 on the Wood Green side of the park was destroyed by fire. Older than the palace, this building had also been used as workshops by parachutists, had been converted into the Tudor Ballroom with a new dance floor, and during the Second World War had been rented by a clothing firm. From these last tenants the building took its final name of Blandford Hall. In 1964 materials for the Shakespeare quatercentenary celebrations had been made within it. No trace of the building remains on the site, but the nearby path is still known as Blandford Road.

Improvements by the GLC included a rebuilt children's playground near The Avenue, a boating lake hut, upgrading of the pitch and putt course, a ski slope and a collection of animals to form a children's zoo near the Alexandra Park Road pedestrian entrance. At this time a miniature railway still circled the boating lake, giving both adults and children leisure rides. New children's facilities were also provided in the Grove.

In 1970 the Jockey Club would not renew the race track licence as the course did not meet modern horse-racing requirements, and the end of an era of racing had to be accepted. The 1865 grandstand was demolished. Donkey Derby fun events had been run latterly for charity causes on the race course, with the rising young actress Kate O'Mara opening one event.

In November 1974 the roller-skating rink was closed because of a dangerous roof. Exhibitions continued to be held in the Palace. For the spring bank holiday in May 1975 a centenary event celebrated the 100th anniversary of the building. The GLC had continued with repairs to patch up the palace, but the building required more and more expenditure on restoration and maintenance.

Banquet hall built in the park in 1864. Converted into the Tudor Ballroom in 1921 and into Blandford Hall clothing works during the second world war. Destroyed by fire in 1971. (Courtesy of Roy Tremlett).

Haringey council acquires the palace and park

Haringey council had been disappointed that it had not been given responsibility for Alexandra Palace and Park, as they lay wholly within the borough's boundaries. In February 1979 Haringey designated Alexandra Palace and Park a Conservation Area following the secretary of state's refusal in 1978 to 'list' the building himself. Negotiations with the GLC to take over were undertaken in 1979 and successfully concluded. Acquisition in January 1980 was helped by a GLC 'dowry' of £8.5m to help restore the palace.

Plans were devised by Haringey council to develop the building. Further expansion of the commercial exhibition side was seen as the way in which the palace might become profitable, coupled with conference facilities. Before the takeover a booklet was published by Haringey in October 1979 outlining detailed proposals. A consultative committee with representatives of local residents associations and other groups was formed.

The second Alexandra Palace fire put a sudden stop to the discussions. On the afternoon of July 10th 1980 a fire began in the area of the organ (its cause never satisfactorily explained) and, fanned by a wind, spread west across the building. When the spectacular conflagration was put out that night (they were the tallest flames I had ever seen) the great Hall was a ruin and the western side severely damaged. Fortunately there were no casualties.

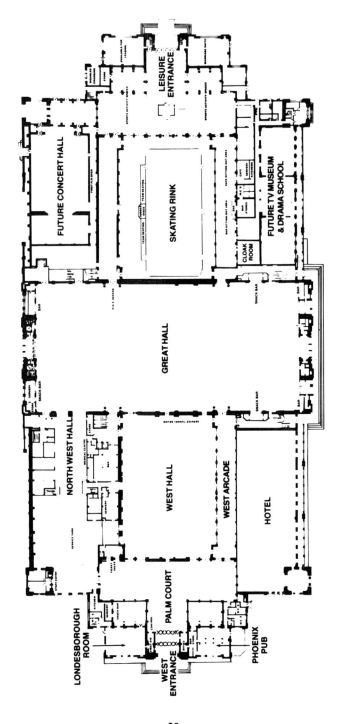

Plan for 1980s restoration. *The exhibition halls, Palm Court and west entrance areas were opened in 1988, and the skating rink in 1990. The rest of the palace remained to be restored in 1992.*

30

Haringey decided to rebuild within the surviving walls. To the £8.5m GLC 'dowry' was added £18.5m insurance money to give, with interest of some £15m, a total of £42m of which £35.4m was to be allocated as the rebuilding budget. To maintain activities the council erected the large, temporary Alexandra Pavilion on the site of a disused bowling green and boxing club hut on the east side of the palace. This metal, canvas and plastic structure was to be well-used — among others by Clive Sinclair to demonstrate his ill-fated 'C5' electrically assisted pedal cycle.

The idea of a major exhibition complex on their doorsteps was resisted by some local residents who formed the Save Our Space (SOS) group to campaign against it. The result was a public enquiry lasting from February to July 1982. The recommendation of the inspector, Mr MI Montague-Smith in March 1983 was that Haringey's development application be granted planning permission, with the exception of a proposed car park on the football field which backed on Alexandra Park Road houses. The inspector made other recommendations, including the setting up of a small advisory committee representing local people to monitor and control activities. This was included in the subsequent Alexandra Park and Palace Act 1985 which also reinforced the trustees' statutory duty to uphold and repair the palace and to maintain it and the park as a place of public resort and recreation.

The inspector recommended that the Alexandra Pavilion be removed when the palace had been brought back into use and its site used as an additional car park. This was undertaken in July 1990 when in the absence of any other purchase offers the pavilion was sold for scrap.

Restoration and redesign of the palace was carried out by an architectural team under Dr Peter Smith, employed by Haringey. Much research was undertaken to discover the original Victorian architectural features of the building and restoration aimed to keep the palace in Victorian style. Contractors Taylor Woodrow completed the first phase of the restoration in 1988. In March the exhibition halls were officially opened. Second phase work culminated in the opening of an ice-skating rink in the east end of the building in July 1990.

The east end of the building had been the part leased by the BBC. After the second world war many notable pioneering television programmes were broadcast from here. Many famous names in entertainment, politics and other fields made their way to the television studios. Although a new BBC Television Centre was created at White City the palace continued to be leased by the BBC and was used for the twice-weekly newsreel which went out under the sign of the Alexandra Palace mast. As technology changed, the BBC made over parts of its leased area to the programme makers for the new Open University, until the OU was consolidated in Milton Keynes. Another palace tenant was Middlesex Polytechnic, which used a southern section, formerly the Badminton Suite, as part of Hornsey Art School. The fire destroyed this part of the building and the polytechnic moved to premises nearby in Quicksilver Place, Wood Green.

Aerial view of restored palace showing the new roof to the great hall and the temporary Alexandra Pavilion.
(Courtesy of Alexandra Palace & Park).

32

Redevelopment also included the park. New trees were planted and other landscape work undertaken with a nature conservation area developed on the east side for educational purposes. A lakeside boathouse (with toilets) was built. Extensive new car parks were opened in 1985 on the site of the former race track paddocks. Commercial nurseries (Stroud Nurseries) near the Grove were replaced by a garden centre, opened 8th March 1986. The Dukes Avenue pedestrian entrance (which for a time had been used as a road) was redesigned and won a Civic Trust award for the result. The disused railway station was renovated and made into a community centre run by a group called CUFOS (Community Use for the Old Station). The north side of the palace, used for car auctions for some years, was tidied up and made into a service car park.

As with nearly all capital projects the cost of carrying out the work exceeded the estimates. Insufficient funds existed to complete the rebuilding programme. It had been intended to have a television museum preserving the unique pioneering studios; a base for the local astronomical society on one of the towers; a preserved and revitalised Victorian theatre, possibly used for concerts or recordings; and a hotel in the south-west corner. One hotel company was contracted to develop the latter but the attempt proved abortive due to space and planning permission problems. Restoration of the organ still depended on the response to the organ appeal. Plans for a drama school (the Mountview) to occupy an important southern part of the palace were delayed. Above all, the cost of the reconstruction of park and palace exceeded the money available by about £30m. Responsibility for the overspend was disputed.

Lack of capital resources by Haringey Council and the trustees to continue the planned palace developments, and the immense problem caused by the over-spend and consequent debt led the palace trustees (all Haringey councillors) to take a radical new examination of future plans. A development brief prepared for the trustees by KPMG Management Consulting, published in 1991, invited expressions of interest from developers to lease palace and park. Four companies were shortlisted from some 30 replies, and three submitted detailed proposals. Those put forward by Powerhouse 91 (connected with the national company Tarmac) were chosen by the trustees for consideration on 26th October 1991.

Local residents, fearful of the impact of commercial entrepreneurship on the local environment, both within and without the park, formed in October 1991 STOPP (Save the Open Parkland and Palace) 'an umbrella group to coordinate the campaign against the loss of open green space in Alexandra Park and the preservation of the historic features of Alexandra Palace'. The protest initiative sought to prevent unacceptable commercial development. Free use of the park as an open space was a particular concern as well as the prevention of excessive traffic, leading to parking on neighbouring streets, noise and other environmental problems. Saving the historic television studios and the Victorian theatre were also important concerns.

In December 1991 Haringey Council decided that implementation of Powerhouse 91 proposals should be postponed until the issue of the £30m rebuilding debt was resolved. This was following the intervention of the Attorney General who advised the borough solicitor that arbritration should decide whether the council or the charitable trust for the Palace should repay the debt. Arbritration proceedings are likely to take at least one year.

Despite the financial woes, and disagreements over the way the building and park should serve the populace, the great hulk of Alexandra Palace, set in its own parkland, remains on its hill, for many people a reminder of countless happy occasions. Its park of nearly 200 acres has always been a valuable open space, whether for rallies, gatherings and entertainments, or as a quiet place of relaxation where nature can be enjoyed by urban dwellers. A tribute is due to Owen Jones who conceived it, and to the many people who helped its survival. Its familiar shape on the skyline is a reminder of a great historical legacy.

FURTHER READING

The only relevant full length book is *Alexandra Park & Palace* by Ron Carrington (GLC 1975), published to mark the centenary of the second building. I have been indebted to this volume for many facts relating to Palace history. Unfortunately it is now out of print, as is *Alexandra Palace & Park* by Dr Peter Smith. This nine page pamphlet, published by Hornsey Historical Society, and written by the architect of the palace restoration, was originally an article in an HHS *Bulletin. Lost Houses of Haringey* (1986), produced jointly by the Borough of Haringey and Hornsey Historical Society, contains a researched article by Dr Joan Schwitzer giving the history of the Grove.

The history of railways to the Palace is well described in *London's Local Railways* by Alan A. Jackson (David & Charles 1978) and I have found this book invaluable. A later pamphlet on the same subject is *Ally Pally: The Alexandra Palace – Its Transport and Its Troubles* by CT Goode (Forge Books 1983). *Rails to the People's Palace* by Reg Davies (HHS, 2nd ed. 1985) gives a history and description of the line from Finsbury Park to Alexandra Palace. I found John R. Kellett's *Railways and Victorian Cities* (Routledge & Kegan Paul 1969) useful background reading.

Details of the 1862 exhibition are to be found in the *Survey of London vol. XXXVIII, South Kensington – The Museum Area* (Athlone Press 1975). Information about the Crystal Palace is to be found in *Palace of the People* by Graham Reeves, a booklet published by Bromley Library Services in 1986. *The Great Exhibition of 1851,* a Victoria and Albert Museum booklet (HMSO, 2nd ed. 1981), describes this great event. The career of parachutist Dolly Shepherd is outlined in *When the Chute Went Up* by Dolly Shepherd and Peter Hearn (Robert Hale 1984).

From Highgate to Hornsey by Ken Gay and Dick Whetstone (SB Publications 1988) includes 17 views of the palace and park in Edwardian times, with explanatory captions. Two more views and further local information are given in *In Times Past - Wood Green and Tottenham with West Green and Harringay* by Peter Curtis (HHS 1991).

For those interested in the history of the surrounding area a number of publications are available from Hornsey Historical Society. These include *From Forest to Suburb - the story of Hornsey retold* by Ken Gay (HHS 1986) and the pocket-sized *A Walk Around Muswell Hill* (HHs 1986), text by Ken Gay. The society publishes a wide range of black and white period postcards, including some of the Palace as well as four modern colour postards of th Palace as it was in 1990. Copies of the 1894 Ordnance Survey 6 inch map, the first to show the Palace, are also available.

The official anniversary of public television is given as November 2, 1937 but the significant date was February 5, 1938 when the Marconi-EMI system became established as the single system of transmission in preference to the Baird. The staff engaged in "turning an ingenious toy into a serious entertainment" was based at Alexandra Palace and numbered about 260.

ONE TELEVISION YEAR

GROWING PAINS

From Our Special Correspondent

Gaunt and unlovely, the Palace dominates part of North London with only the 220ft mast to indicate the marvel in the south-east corner. An inadvertent entry by the back door brings the visitor over a desolate branch terminus of the L.N.E.R. (London and North-Eastern Railway) into empty, echoing halls, where the assorted objects might have been gathered by a surrealist. Sections of stuffed lions, slot-machines, a bar, posters of dance competitions, and a statue of Lincoln are distributed haphazard. Only a discreet grey door in a corner, painted "No entry", marks the back entrance to the overcrowded hive of television. Here the essentials are in the vision and sound transmitting halls on the ground floor, and in two studios above them.

On the other side of a narrow corridor, which is both artery and boulevard, are the make-up and dressing rooms, and on the ground floor is a small restaurant. The executive staff's rooms are in the east tower, and in the north-west corner of the building, separated from the rest by the Winter Garden, is the carpenter's shop and an old theatre which the station has acquired with an open mind.

The station's day has two feverish campaigns, culminating at 3 o'clock in the afternoon and 9 o'clock in the evening. The piano-tuner has to arrive at 7am because there is no room for him later. The morning is filled with rehearsals and a film demonstration for the benefit of the radio trade and rehearsals have to be juggled in and out of the two stages. For the convenience of artists, some early ones take place at Broadcasting House or Maida Vale; if the artists came to the station more frequently they might find no space to rehearse in. When a condensed *Othello* was performed recently there was only one two-hour rehearsal on the stage. The actress who played Desdemona had never seen a television camera before, so that she had little enough time to learn how to act *into* the camera or to master the art of two-dimensional gesture. (A lovely movement of appealing arms stretched towards the camera misses its effect if the arms leap out of focus into the semblance of giant marrows.)

The prevalent spirit was expressed by the studio hand who said, "We're not working; we're being paid for a hobby." With no precedents, no cramping case law, the station experiments like a bunch of earnest schoolboys. This, doubtless, was the spirit of Savoy Hill in the early days, and it is bound to be lost ultimately, but in the interval a number of people are having the time of their lives. Technically the range of the individual service, using ultra-short waves, will continue to have an outside limit of 40 miles.

It is not unfair to presume that there would be many more buyers if the daily service were longer than two hours, but the BBC is temporarily at its limits of time, space, and money for producing two hours of television, let alone a continuous service. So far England, with the only regular television service, is in this one field of applied science indisputably ahead of the world. This fact, a platitude to anyone who has examined the subject, is curiously unappreciated by the lay public, who are judging an infant as if it were a backward adult.